EYEWITNESS DISASTER
VOLCANOES!

HELEN DWYER

W
FRANKLIN WATTS
LONDON • SYDNEY

First published in 2010 by Franklin Watts

Copyright © 2010 Arcturus Publishing Limited

Franklin Watts
338 Euston Road
London NW1 3BH

Franklin Watts Australia
Level 17/207 Kent Street, Sydney, NSW 2000

Produced by Arcturus Publishing Limited,
26/27 Bickels Yard, 151–153 Bermondsey Street, London SE1 3HA

The right of Helen Dwyer to be identified as the author of this work has been asserted by her in accordance with the Copyright, Designs and Patents Act 1988.

Planned and produced by Discovery Books Ltd., 2 College Street, Ludlow, Shropshire, SY8 1AN www.discoverybooks.net
Managing editor: Rachel Tisdale
Editor: Helen Dwyer
Designer: sprout.uk.com Limited
Illustrator: Stefan Chabluk
Picture researcher: Tom Humphrey

Photo acknowledgements: Corbis: 7 (Frans Lanting), 17, 26 (Roger Ressmeyer), 29 (Reuters). Getty Images: 9 (Bruce Alexander/AFP), 10 (Philippe Bourseiller), 12 (Marco Longari/AFP), 13 (Pedro Ugarte/AFP), 14 (STF/AFP), 15 (Arlan Naeg), 16 (Richard Roscoe/Visuals), 17 (Roberto Campos/AFP), 19 (Astromujoff/The Image Bank), 25 (Science and Society Picture Library), 28 (Rodrigo Buendia/AFP). NASA: 21, 27. Shutterstock: cover (juliengrondin), 4 (Andrea Danti), 5 (juliengrondin), 8 (Sergio B), 11 (Bryan Busovicki), 23 (Katrina Leigh). Wikimedia: 15 (Mediacaster40), 18 (Donald A Swanson/USGS Cascades Volcano Observatory), 24 (Ranveig).

Cover Picture: Volcano erupting

Sources
http://www.cotf.edu/ete/modules/volcanoes/vmtvesuvius.html *page 4*
http://volcanoes.usgs.gov/ash/ashfall.html *page 9*
http://news.bbc.co.uk/1/hi/sci/tech/7950845.stm *page 11*
http://www.independent.co.uk/news/world/africa/fears-for-goma-over-new-volcano-threat-573555.html *page 12*
http://www.rainforestportal.org/shared/reader/welcome.aspx?linkid=6801 *page 12*
http://archives.cnn.com/2002/WORLD/africa/01/19/volcano.quotes/index.html?related *page 12*
http://archives.cnn.com/2002/WORLD/africa/01/19/volcano.quotes/index.html?related *page 13*
http://news.bbc.co.uk/1/hi/world/americas/4231020.stm *page 14*
http://www.geology.sdsu.edu/how_volcanoes_work/Pelee.html *page 17*
http://pubs.usgs.gov/gip/msh/debris.html *page 18*
http://www.kgw.com/news-local/stories/kgw_051705_local_helens_witnesses.282891877.html *page 18*
http://news.bbc.co.uk/onthisday/hi/witness/may/19/newsid_3708000/3708361.stm *page 18*
Jón Steingrímsson, translated by Keneva Kunz. *The Laki Eruption 1783–1784.* University of Iceland Press, 1998 *page 20*
http://modernhistorian.blogspot.com/2008_06_01_archive.html *page 21*
http://www.guardian.co.uk/science/2005/aug/18/farout *page 21*
http://www.cfa.harvard.edu/~wsoon/1816-Mercury03-d/Summer_of_1816.pdf *page 22*
http://www.theatlantic.com/issues/1884sep/sturdy.htm *page 24*
http://dsc.discovery.com/convergence/krakatoa/diaries/lindeman.html *page 24*
http://www.pbs.org/wgbh/nova/volcano/chouet.html *page 27*
http://news.bbc.co.uk/1/hi/sci/tech/282092.stm *page 29*

The website addresses (URLs) included in this book (here and in the resources section on page 31) were valid at the time of going to press. However, because of the nature of the Internet, it is possible that some addresses may have changed, or the sites may have changed or closed down since publication. While the author, packager and the publisher regret any inconvenience this may cause to the readers, no responsibility for any such changes can be accepted by the author, packager or publisher.

Words in **bold type** or underlined appear in the glossary on page 30.

A CIP catalogue record for this publication is available from the British Library.

Dewey classification number: 363.3'495

ISBN 978 1 4451 0063 0

Printed in China

Franklin Watts is a division of Hachette Children's Books, an Hachette UK Company.
www.hachette.co.uk

CONTENTS

WHAT IS A VOLCANO?

A volcano is a hill or mountain, often conical-shaped, with an opening in the middle. The opening extends down into chambers of liquid rock deep inside the earth. This rock is called **magma**. It is less **dense** than solid rock and full of hot gases so it rises up towards the earth's surface. When it reaches weak areas or cracks in the solid rocks above it, the magma breaks through, or erupts.

In an active volcano, magma pushes up through weak points in the earth's rocks and then through the volcano mound itself. The mound is made of layers of material from previous eruptions.

'[The cloud looked] like a pine . . . for it rose to a great height on a sort of trunk and then split off into branches . . . Sometimes it looked white, sometimes blotched and dirty, according to the amount of soil and ashes it carried with it . . . On Mount Vesuvius broad sheets of fire and leaping flames blazed.'

Pliny the Younger describes the eruption of Vesuvius, Italy, in 79 CE. This is the first written description of a volcanic eruption.

Magma

Volcanic ash, rocks and lava from previous eruptions

Solid rock

When a volcano erupts, the liquid magma may flow down its sides, or it may explode into the air.

VOLCANO LEGENDS

The word *volcano* comes from a small island of that name off the coast of southern Italy. The ancient Romans believed it was the home of their blacksmith god Vulcan. They thought that the island's volcano was the chimney of Vulcan's workshop and that the volcano's eruptions were a sign that Vulcan was busy working.

The people of the Hawaiian Islands believed a goddess named Pele triggered volcanic eruptions by digging the ground with a magic stick when she was angry.

In the 12th century, a volcano called Hekla became active in Iceland. People in Europe believed that Hekla was the entrance to Hell and that the pieces of **lava** that flew hissing through the air were the souls of people screaming in pain.

Eruption patterns

Some volcanoes erupt regularly while others lie dormant (sleeping) for hundreds or even thousands of years. Volcanic eruptions are taking place all the time, but often they are in areas with few people, such as Alaska in North America or Siberia in eastern Russia. Fortunately, eruptions rarely cause large-scale human disasters.

WHERE CAN VOLCANOES BE FOUND?

Volcanoes only occur in certain places. The earth's outermost layer – the **crust** – is like a shell made up of lots of large, hard blocks that move about very slowly above a hotter, softer layer called the **mantle**.

These blocks are called **tectonic plates**. Most volcanic activity takes place along plate edges, especially the area around the Pacific Ocean, which is known as the Pacific Ring of Fire.

This world map shows how volcanoes (red circles) occur near or on tectonic plate edges (white lines). The pink band – where most volcanoes are located – covers an area known as the Pacific Ring of Fire. The blue band is the area known as the Mid-Atlantic Ridge, where plates are pulling apart. At its northern end are the volcanoes that formed Iceland. The arrows on the map show which way the larger plates are moving.

Plate movements

Some plate boundaries are pulling apart (diverging) from each other on the ocean floor. The space left as they separate is filled by magma which rises from below, then cools and hardens. The Mid-Atlantic Ridge, which runs from north to south through the Atlantic Ocean, is a divergent boundary with many volcanoes.

Other plate boundaries collide with each other (converge). Usually an oceanic plate is forced down (subducted) below a continental plate. As it is forced down to a depth of about 100 kilometres the oceanic plate starts to melt, forming new magma. This magma escapes through the crust, creating volcanoes on the edges of continents.

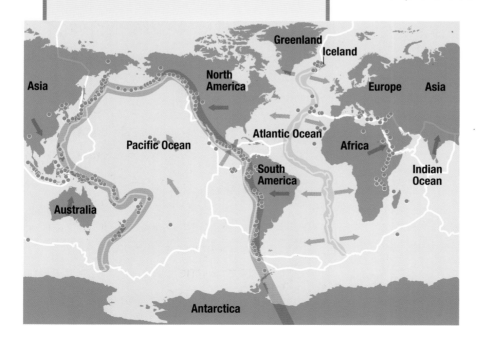

Greenland
Iceland
Asia
North America
Europe
Asia
Atlantic Ocean
Africa
Pacific Ocean
South America
Indian Ocean
Australia
Antarctica

The Galápagos islands in the Pacific Ocean formed from volcanic activity above a mantle plume. As the tectonic plate moves above the plume, new volcanoes are formed. This photo shows volcanic craters on the island of Isabela.

RISING FROM THE SEA

New volcanoes are still being created in the oceans. In Hawaii, Loi'hi Seamount began forming around 400,000 years ago. It has now risen 3,000 metres above the sea floor but it is not likely to break the ocean surface for at least 10,000 years.

In 1963 undersea volcanic eruptions created a new island called Surtsey, near the coast of Iceland. Surtsey continued to erupt and grow until 1967. Since then it has been worn away by the sea to an area of 1.4 square kilometres – about half the size it was in 1967.

Hotspots

Some volcanoes occur away from plate boundaries in areas known as **hotspots**. These can be found above mantle plumes, which are columns of hot rock that rise through the earth's mantle and into the crust. The crust then melts, forming channels through which magma can escape. As the tectonic plates above move, the mantle plume stays in the same place. So, over millions of years, new volcanoes are formed and old ones become extinct. The Galápagos and Hawaiian islands were formed in this way.

TYPES OF ERUPTIONS

Red-hot lava flows from Mount Etna in Sicily. Etna is one of the most active volcanoes in the world, yet people still farm on the fertile soil at its base.

Volcanoes erupt in different ways. Eruptions can be gentle or explosive, depending on the sort of magma in the volcano. As magma rises, the gas bubbles inside it expand to hundreds of times their original size.

Types of magma

If the magma is very runny liquid, the gases escape easily into the air, and the magma simply flows down the sides of the volcano. Once it is outside the volcano, this type of magma is known as lava.

If the magma is thick, the expanding gases are trapped. Eventually the pressure in the magma triggers an explosion as the gases force their way out. Magma is blasted into the air and breaks up into pieces. These fragments are called **tephra** and they range in size from small particles of ash to large boulders. Both lava and tephra become solid as they cool.

'The ash was mushrooming out in thick clouds [which] began to drift towards us. The sky was darkening and black specks of ash were falling on us. There was an overpowering smell of sulphur.'

One eyewitness's experience of an eruption in Papua New Guinea, 1994.

Gas dangers

The gases from a volcano can be as deadly as lava and ash. They can poison people or animals nearby. If they rise high into the atmosphere they may mix with moisture to create **acid rain** or they may block out heat and light from the sun.

Pacific islanders watch from a safe distance as Tavurvur volcano sends clouds of ash over the town of Rabaul, Papua New Guinea, in 2006.

AMAZING ESCAPE

Inside an ash cloud

In 1982, Galunggung volcano in Indonesia erupted. About 150 kilometres away, the crew and passengers on a British aircraft saw flashes of glowing light and the plane was filled with the smell of **sulphur dioxide**. The plane was enveloped in a volcanic ash cloud. Ash melted on the jet engines, which stopped working. The plane glided slowly downwards – 7,000 metres in 16 minutes. Then – as some of the cooled ash broke off – the engines began to work again and the plane landed safely.

Following an eruption

When hot volcanic material meets water, snow or ice, it mixes with it to form mudslides. **Landslides** can also follow volcanic eruptions. Underwater eruptions sometimes cause shock waves called **tsunamis**, which spread out across the ocean and break as giant waves on coasts.

FLOWING LAVA

The volcanoes of Hawaii and Iceland are known as shield volcanoes because their low, curved shape resembles a shield. This shape is created by liquid lava flowing a long distance from the vent (opening) in all directions before it cools and turns to rock. The slopes of shield volcanoes are quite gentle, so the lava moves fairly slowly. Shield volcanoes are generally not explosive. When they erupt they eject mainly molten lava. The lava can destroy property, but usually people have time to get out of its path.

Volcanoes on Hawaii

Hawaii's volcanoes are monitored round the clock, and people are rarely hurt by the erupting lava. Kilauea is the most active volcano in the world. It has been erupting regularly since 1983.

Lava and ash

In other parts of the world, volcanoes produce a mixture of lava and more solid material and are made up of layers of lava, ash and rocks. Mount Etna in Sicily is one of these. Lava from Etna often threatens villages on its slopes.

Lava lakes

Very rarely, lakes of molten lava build up in the craters of volcanoes. Today there are

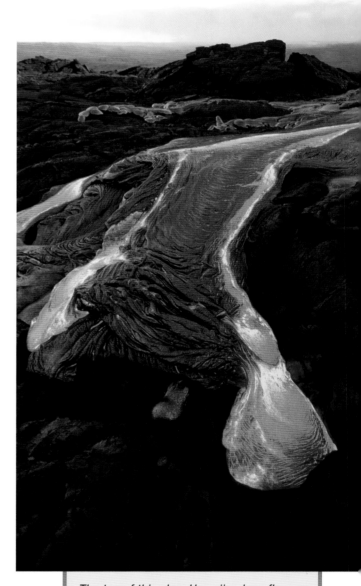

The top of this slow Hawaiian lava flow is beginning to cool and darken as it is exposed to the air. The lava underneath remains much hotter.

five lava lakes in the world. Two are in Africa's Great Rift Valley, where the earth's crust is pulling apart. One of these, Erta Ale in Ethiopia, has been erupting continuously since 1967.

' The incandescent [glowing] bubbling lava lake hisses like some badly burned porridge cauldron, overturning and occasionally belching molten lava.'

Earth scientist Dr Dougal Jerram, describing the lava lake in Erta Ale, Ethiopia.

Red-hot lava glows through a hole in a lava tube in Hawaii.

LAVA TUBES

Sometimes a stream of fluid lava cools and forms a crust on its top surface. Eventually the other surfaces may also cool to form a hollow tube. Liquid lava flows through this tube, but because it is surrounded by the newly solidified rock of the tube walls, its heat is trapped. The lava remains much hotter and more liquid – and also flows more quickly – than if it was exposed to the air. This makes it much more dangerous than ordinary lava, so sometimes people try to destroy lava tubes with explosives.

'All I see is burning trees and fire.'
NYIRAGONGO, DEMOCRATIC REPUBLIC OF CONGO 2002

People in the city of Goma described the lava flows from Mount Nyiragongo.

'The ground started shaking and fire came out.'
Furazh Kiza, Goma resident

'I've never seen so much fire in my life. I look up at the volcano and all I see is burning trees and fire.'
Karine Morency, United Nations worker

'Most of the town has been ... buried under thick, dense black mud [lava] which is hardening like concrete.'
Alison Preston, aid worker

Mount Nyiragongo is Africa's most dangerous volcano. It has been created by the African tectonic plate tearing apart. On 17 January 2002 a **fissure** opened up and spread 13 kilometres down the volcano and across the plain to the edge of the city of Goma. Fountains of lava burst out along the fissure and a lava river – at times more than one kilometre wide and two metres high – spilled through the city, dividing it in two.

A young boy walks past smoking lava in Goma. About 50 people died from the poisonous gases coming from the lava.

HELPING HANDS

The tragedy in Goma left many people with burns that needed treatment. The **aid agency** Médecins Sans Frontières supplied burns kits to the hospital in Goma, which, fortunately, was unaffected by the lava. These kits contained bandages, **anaesthetics** to relieve pain, **antibiotics** to prevent the burns becoming infected, and serum (a watery fluid) to help people who had become **dehydrated**.

Destruction in Goma

The people of Goma fled the lava as it destroyed their homes. The lava – and the earthquakes that followed – wrecked thousands of buildings and left 120,000 people homeless. Around 100 people died in the disaster.

The future

The volcano is still very active and scientists fear that the next eruption could be under the city itself. Even worse, it might be under nearby Lake Kiva, where it could set loose a cloud of poisonous gases – including **carbon dioxide** and **hydrogen sulphide** – which could kill millions of people.

' There is no water, no food, no shelter. Some people are feeling sick because of the smoke. Children are hungry.'

Themis Hakizimana, photographer at Goma.

A petrol station explodes in Goma after burning lava set fire to the petrol.

RIVERS OF MUD

When ash and fragments of rock from a volcano mix with water, snow or ice they sometimes create mudslides or landslides called **lahars**. This muddy mixture is very fluid so it can travel downhill at great speed, but when it settles it becomes solid like cement. Volcanic mudslides kill many more people than lava does.

The tragedy of Armero

In 1985, the volcano Nevado del Ruiz erupted in Colombia. Hot ash and gas melted the snow and **glaciers** on the summit, creating several lahars that raced at 60 kph down into the river valleys on the volcano's sides.

' There was a lot of confusion. People were in shock. Hundreds of people were trapped. I could hear people screaming for help and then silence – an eerie silence.'

A photographer described the scene three days after the mudslide in Armero, 1985.

One of these lahars wiped out the riverside town of Armero. Eighty per cent of the people died under the mud and almost all of the survivors were injured. Unfortunately a storm had cut electricity to Armero, and radio broadcasts warning them the mudflow was coming never reached the people in the town.

Mount Pinatubo

In 1991, Mount Pinatubo erupted in the Philippines. Although this was the second largest eruption of the 20th century, it had been predicted, so tens of thousands of people moved away from the area. Unfortunately, a major storm followed the eruption and rain mixed with the volcanic ash. The mudslides that followed killed 1,500 people.

The town of Armero, Colombia, lies under muddy water after mudslides from Nevado del Ruiz volcano struck it without warning in 1985.

AMAZING ESCAPE

Saved by chocolate

After Nevado del Ruiz volcano erupted and triggered the Armero mudslide, volunteers dug through the mud looking for survivors. For a whole week they rescued people from the mud, but after that there were no more signs of life. Then in early December, Red Cross workers noticed smoke coming from the rubble. They dug down to find 75-year-old Maria Rosa Echeverri, still in her house by her cooking fire. She had survived for 24 days on rice and chocolate.

Clouds of ash and steam erupt from Mount Pinatubo in 1991. The unexpected mudslides that followed proved more dangerous than the volcanic ash clouds.

ASH AND GAS FLOWS

One of the most deadly results of a volcanic eruption is called a **pyroclastic flow**. This is a cloud of super-hot ash, gases and rocks ejected from a volcano. The cloud stays just above the ground and can travel downhill at more than 700 kph. Anyone caught in a pyroclastic flow will either be burnt to death by the heat or suffocated by the gases and ash.

Mount Vesuvius

The Roman cities of Pompeii and Herculaneum were destroyed by pyroclastic flows from Mount Vesuvius in 79 CE. In Herculaneum, which was closer to the volcano, people were burnt to death. Further

away in Pompeii, the flow was not as hot but people there were suffocated by ash.

The death of Saint-Pierre

The worst pyroclastic flow disaster in history occurred on the Caribbean island of Martinique in 1902. An eruption ripped open the top of Mount Pelée and a thick, black cloud of steam, gases and ash was released. This pyroclastic flow was hotter than 1,000°C and moved at a speed of 670 kph. In seconds it had covered the city

This pyroclastic flow is from the volcano on the Caribbean island of Montserrat during an eruption in 2006.

of Saint-Pierre, 6.5 kilometres away, setting fire to the buildings. The city burned for many days. Of the population of 30,000, only two men survived.

> ' I felt a terrible wind blowing, the earth began to tremble and the sky became suddenly dark. I . . . felt my arms and legs burning.'
>
> Léon Compère-Léandre, survivor of the Mount Pelée eruption, 1902.

AMAZING ESCAPE

The man who lived through doomsday

The luckiest man in Saint-Pierre was in a windowless, underground prison cell when the volcano erupted. Louis Cyparis was waiting for breakfast when it suddenly grew very dark. Hot air mixed with fine ashes came through the barred window in the door and burned him. Cyparis jumped in agony about the cell and cried for help. He was found by rescuers four days later and set free. He joined an American circus as 'The Man Who Lived Through Doomsday', sitting in a replica of his prison cell and telling visitors about his experience.

The streets of Esquel, Argentina, were covered in a thick layer of volcanic ash when Chaitén volcano in Chile erupted in May 2008. People wore masks to avoid breathing the ash.

'The whole north side of the summit crater began to move.'

MOUNT ST HELENS 1980

People who were near to Mount St Helens when it erupted spoke about their experiences.

' 'The whole north side of the summit crater began to move . . . The entire mass began to ripple and churn up.'
Keith and Dorothy Soffel, flying over the volcano as it erupted

'It was just billowing . . . within [the] grey plume were white steam clouds, and there was lightning striking.'
Valerie Pierson, forest ranger

'It was pitch black dark, the air was so thick with ash and smoke you couldn't see a foot [30 centimetres] in front of yourself. We were being pelted with what looked like huge globes of mud.'
Jamie Walt, camper '

Mount St Helens is a volcano in the Cascade Mountains of Washington State in the United States. Since the middle of the 19th century, this snow-capped and forested mountain had been dormant. Then in early 1980 it began to stir, producing earthquakes and eruptions of steam. New craters formed and two fissures appeared on the north side. Most alarming of all, a bulge formed between the fissures and expanded outwards by two metres a day.

Ash from the Mount St Helens eruption was blasted high into the atmosphere and eventually came down in eleven US states.

This photo from above shows the damage caused on the north side of the volcano, which was completely destroyed. The forests on this side of the volcano were also destroyed in the eruption.

As the volcano blew apart, hot ash, rocks and gases erupted from it. They also flowed down the north side, overtaking the landslide.

Mudslides and ash clouds

The hot ash and gases melted snow and glaciers. The mixture of ash and water formed mudslides which travelled 80 kilometres. At the same time, a column of ash escaped from the summit. In only 15 minutes a mushroom-shaped ash cloud rose 24 kilometres into the atmosphere. In all, the eruption killed 57 people and destroyed more than 200 houses.

Blasted apart

On 18 May an enormous sideways eruption blew apart the north side of the volcano where the bulge had been. The boulders and rock fragments became a landslide which covered an area of 60 square kilometres.

ASH CHAOS

In Washington State, the ash was in the air for many days, causing temporary breathing problems for thousands of people. Ash blanketed many farms, destroying the crops, and covered roads and airports. The ash particles in the air made it very difficult to see. They were also a disaster for machinery of all sorts. The ash particles found their way into engines, machines and electrical equipment, clogging them up and scratching moving parts.

DEADLY POISONS

Volcanoes release a mixture of gases, which can have a major impact on people and the environment. For example, sulphur dioxide mixes with water to form acid rain. People downwind of a volcano will often experience acid rain for a time after an eruption.

Laki erupts

In June 1783, Laki volcano in Iceland erupted, ejecting million of tons of **hydrogen fluoride** and sulphur dioxide. The hydrogen fluoride settled on plants and grass and was eaten by farm animals.

'More poison fell from the sky than words can describe . . . The snouts, nostrils and feet of animals turned bright yellow and raw. All the earth's plants burned, withered and turned grey.'

Jón Steingrímsson, parish priest near Laki, 1783–1784.

The animals' joints became deformed so they could not walk, and their teeth grew uncontrollably. More than half the livestock in Iceland died. Around a quarter of the population died too – of fluorine and sulphur dioxide poisoning and of starvation.

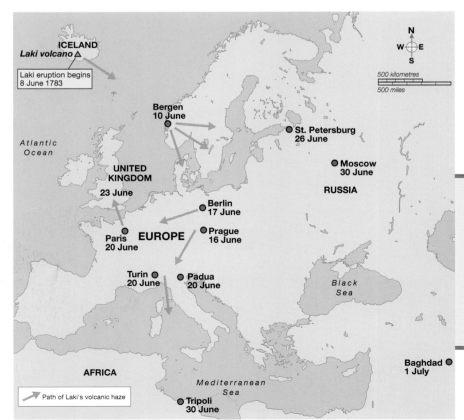

This map shows how quickly the poisonous fog from Laki reached Europe, western Asia and northern Africa. The fog lasted until October and was followed by a very cold winter.

The Laki haze

Just days after Laki erupted, a sulphurous fog reached Europe. English poet William Cowper wrote: '(People) are indisposed by fevers . . . the labourers (are) carried out of the fields incapable of work and many die.' Death records in Britain show thousands more people than usual died between August and October 1783.

> 'The sun, at noon, looked as blank as a clouded moon and shed a rust-coloured light on the ground . . . the heat was so intense that meat could hardly be eaten on the day after it was killed.'
>
> *From the diary of British **naturalist** Gilbert White, summer 1783.*

Killer carbon dioxide

Carbon dioxide gas can be a killer, too. Lake Nyos in Cameroon, western Africa, lies on the side of a volcano. Magma beneath the lake gives off carbon dioxide, which leaks into the water. In 1986 a large cloud of carbon dioxide was suddenly released from the lake. It rolled down two nearby valleys, suffocating 1,700 people.

HAWAIIAN VOG

Today in Hawaii, Kilauea volcano often releases sulphur dioxide. When the gas forms particles in the air it creates a haze that the islanders call vog – short for 'volcanic smog'. People nearby suffer from breathing problems such as bronchitis (lung inflammation).

A photo, taken from a space shuttle, shows Hawaiian islands hidden by a volcanic haze.

GOING GLOBAL

There is plenty of evidence to show that a single volcanic eruption can affect the earth's climate. For example, the largest volcanic eruption ever recorded was from Mount Tambora in Indonesia in April 1815. The gases and ash from Tambora reached a height of 43 kilometres. Winds spread the ash particles around the world.

The year without a summer

The eruption led to the following year, 1816, being known as 'the year without a summer'. In North America, northern Europe and China, there were frosts and snowstorms in May and June. Crops throughout North American, Europe and Asia were ruined. Thousands of people starved or were so weakened that they died from disease **epidemics**.

> ' Ground frozen hard,
> and squalls of snow . . .
> icicles 12 inches
> [30 centimetres] long
> in the shade at noon day.'

From the 7 June 1816 weather records of Edward Holyoke in New Hampshire, United States.

This map highlights the effects of the Tambora eruption across the world in 1816. Temperatures everywhere were lower than normal, especially in the vast northern continents.

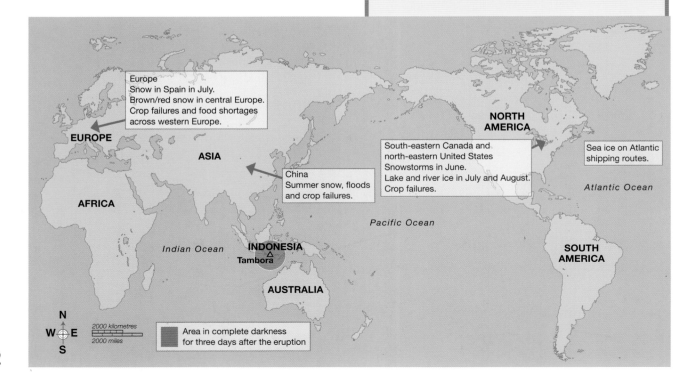

Europe
Snow in Spain in July.
Brown/red snow in central Europe.
Crop failures and food shortages across western Europe.

EUROPE

ASIA

China
Summer snow, floods and crop failures.

AFRICA

NORTH AMERICA

South-eastern Canada and north-eastern United States
Snowstorms in June.
Lake and river ice in July and August.
Crop failures.

Sea ice on Atlantic shipping routes.

Atlantic Ocean

Pacific Ocean

Indian Ocean

INDONESIA
△ Tambora

SOUTH AMERICA

AUSTRALIA

N
W E
S

2000 kilometres
2000 miles

Area in complete darkness for three days after the eruption

In Yellowstone National Park today, the heat in the earth is clearly visible in the daily eruptions of its geysers (hot springs shooting out steam) and mud pots (pools of bubbling mud).

YELLOWSTONE CALDERA

Yellowstone National Park in Wyoming, USA, was the scene of a super volcano eruption 640,000 years ago. When the magma chamber emptied, the land above it collapsed into the space the magma left. This type of land feature is called a **caldera**.

If there were to be another Yellowstone eruption of a similar size to the last one, most of North America would be covered with ash, the world's climate would be affected and people would be unable to grow enough food. However, the scientists who study Yellowstone do not see any sign of that happening at the moment.

Super volcanoes

Eruptions like Tambora do not occur very often, at most once every one or two thousand years. However, scientists have found evidence of much bigger volcanic eruptions in the past. They believe that there have been four **super volcanoes** – ten times the size of Tambora – in the last million years. For example, about 75,000 years ago, ash from a volcano in Indonesia caused a global winter that lasted for a thousand years and killed most of the people on earth. Now scientists are studying the world's volcanoes to find out where the next super eruption will take place.

'The wind...was hot and choking.'

KRAKATOA, INDONESIA 26 AND 27 AUGUST 1883

Many people aboard ships near Krakatoa later described their experiences.

' [Krakatoa] became visible. Chains of fire appeared to ascend and descend between it and the sky. The wind . . . was hot and choking . . . with a smell as of burning cinders [ash].'
Captain Watson on a British ship

'A dense rain of mud fell . . . which made breathing difficult . . . the devilish smell of sulphurous acid spread. Some felt buzzing in the ears, others felt a pressing on the chest and sleepiness. It would have been quite natural if we had all choked to death.'
N H van Sandick, passenger on a ship nearby

Krakatoa was a small island in the Sunda Strait between the much larger islands of Sumatra and Java (part of Indonesia today). In 1883 it erupted with such violence that the explosions were heard in Australia, 3,000 kilometres away. Shock waves travelled through the air and circled the earth several times.

This illustration of Krakatoa erupting dates from 1888. It is based on the reports of eyewitnesses.

These sketches are of twilight skies in Britain after the eruption of Krakatoa. The artist, William Ascroft, was sketching unusual skies like this right up until 1886. The colours were caused by ash dust in the atmosphere.

AMAZING ESCAPE

Tragedy in Sumatra

When Krakatoa erupted, the Beyerinck family was living in the coastal village of Ketimbang in Sumatra – 40 kilometres across the sea from the volcano. A tsunami struck the village and damaged their house. The family fled to their hillside hut but it was not as safe as they hoped: a pyroclastic flow surged towards them over the sea from Krakatoa. The hut was in its path and fountains of hot ash spurted through the floorboards. The Beyerincks were badly burned and their baby died. Somehow they staggered back to the shore, where they found that all the villages had been swept away in another tsunami. The family was eventually rescued by a passing ship and taken to a hospital.

The power of tsunamis

Pyroclastic flows and showers of hot ash killed many people, but tsunamis proved to be even more deadly. These 30-metre-high ocean waves were triggered by the pyroclastic flows as they dumped their heavier rocks into the sea. The lighter materials and gases were carried on a layer of steam across the ocean to Sumatra, where pyroclastic flows probably killed more than 1,000 people. The tsunamis submerged many small islands, destroyed hundreds of coastal villages in Java and Sumatra and left at least 35,000 people dead.

PREDICTING ERUPTIONS

Before scientists can predict a volcanic eruption they need to know what is happening inside the volcano and recognize the events that come before an eruption. They gather the information they need in several ways.

Taking measurements

Measuring gases is one way. Increases in sulphur dioxide emissions indicate rising magma. If increases are followed by a decline in sulphur dioxide there may be a blockage which might build up pressure in the magma and lead to an explosion.

Changes in the shape of the ground also show that magma is rising. These changes are measured by electronic devices and by comparing **satellite** images. Satellites also produce images which show changes in the heat inside a volcano.

Volcanologists (scientists who study volcanoes) collect gas samples from an opening near the crater rim of Colima volcano in Mexico.

This satellite image is of Chaitén volcano in Chile. Chaitén erupted in May 2008 for the first time in nearly 10,000 years. Artificial colours have been added to make the features clearer. The blue area (top right) is where volcanic ash has settled on the ground.

Warning vibrations

Earth movements always occur before eruptions. These are recorded on a machine called a seismometer, which sends electric signals to a computer. Bernard Chouet, a Swiss scientist, noticed that a certain sort of quake, in which gas pressure causes vibrations, produces a recognizable signal.

Chouet looked at records from Mount St Helens and Nevado del Ruiz in the 1980s and realized that the eruptions could have been predicted by these signals. Using this new information, scientists successfully predicted eruptions at Mount Redoubt, Alaska, in 1989 and at Popocatapetl near Mexico City in 2000.

SCIENTISTS IN DANGER

Volcanologists often risk their lives to find out how volcanoes work and how to predict eruptions. When Mount St Helens erupted in 1980 a young scientist named David Johnston was monitoring the volcano for the US **Geological** Survey in Vancouver, Washington State. He was camping on the north side of the volcano as it erupted. His last radio message was simply 'Vancouver, this is it!' Johnston's body was never found.

' Suddenly you realize the volcano is speaking to you and you understand the language. The volcano is singing its tune . . . The volcano is telling you: "I'm under pressure here. I'm going to blow at the top."'

Bernard Chouet describes his discovery that certain seismic signals indicate a volcano is about to erupt.

FIGHT OR FLIGHT?

There is very little anyone can do to stop a volcanic eruption destroying everything in its path. In just a few cases, people have been able to divert lava flows. For example, in the fishing village of Heimaey in Iceland, the residents used hoses and water pumps to spray sea water onto moving lava. As the lava cooled and solidified, it became a dam, diverting fresh lava into the sea.

Problems in Montserrat

When an explosive eruption is predicted, getting out of the way is usually the only sensible option. On the small Caribbean island of Montserrat, a large volcano has erupted regularly since 1992. Around two-thirds of the population left Montserrat to live on other islands or in the United Kingdom.

HELPING HANDS

The US Geological Survey runs a program which helps other countries when volcanoes threaten. It is called the Volcano Disaster Assistance Program (VDAP). When the VDAP is asked to help, it carefully selects the best scientists and equipment for the job.

When Mount Pinatubo in the Philippines became active in 1991, eight VDAP scientists were sent with monitoring equipment. After they had got the equipment working and analyzed the information from it they realized that an eruption was about to begin. Their warnings led to people being evacuated from the area just in time.

An elderly woman living on the slopes of Tungurahua volcano in Ecuador is evacuated from her ash-covered village by soldiers in February 2008. Tungurahua has been regularly active since 1999.

Eruption warnings

Volcanic activity is now carefully monitored by the Montserrat Volcano Observatory. The information it gathers is used to set changing danger levels for different regions of the island. People are advised not to enter areas where they might be in danger.

'Seeing how all the information ties in with each other, this gives us a detailed picture of what is happening and lets us forecast what is likely in the next hours, days and months.'

Richard Robertson, Director of the Montserrat Volcano Observatory, talking about the information gathered by the observatory.

A volcanologist checks earth movements recorded on a seismograph at Clark Field Air Base near the active Pinatubo volcano in the Philippines, 1991.

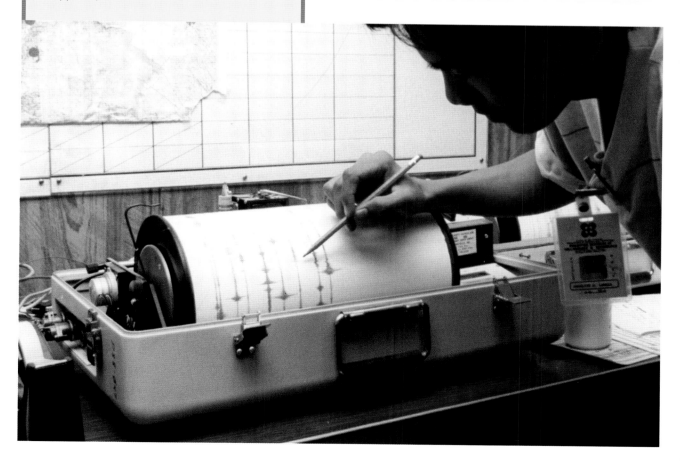

GLOSSARY

acid rain rain made acidic by mixing with sulphur or nitrogen in the air

aid agency an organization that hands out supplies in emergencies

anaesthetics drugs that stop any feeling of pain

antibiotics drugs that kill bacteria

caldera a landscape feature created by land collapsing in a volcanic eruption

carbon dioxide a gas that is poisonous in large quantities and is absorbed by plants

crust the outermost solid layer of the earth, between 5 and 50 kilometres thick

dehydrated having lost too much fluid

dense having parts crowded together

epidemic a disease affecting many people in the same region at the same time

fissure a crack where rocks have split apart

geological concerning the study of the earth's rocks

glacier a slow-moving mass of ice which is formed from layers of crushed snow

hotspot a place on the earth's surface above a mantle plume where volcanic activity occurs regularly

hydrogen fluoride a gas that is extremely poisonous, damaging the lungs and releasing fluorine, which causes bone and tooth damage

hydrogen sulphide a very poisonous gas that is especially dangerous to the nervous system in humans

lahar a mudflow composed of volcanic ash, rocks and water

landslide a fast-moving mass of rocks and debris which rushes down a slope

lava liquid rock after it has left a volcano

magma liquid rock beneath the surface of the earth

mantle the 3,000-kilometre-thick, mainly solid layer of the earth beneath the crust and above the core

naturalist someone who studies plants or animals

pyroclastic flow a cloud of ash, rocks and gas, which erupts from a volcano and flows downhill close to the ground at great speed

satellite an object placed in orbit around the earth

sulphur dioxide a gas which smells of rotten eggs, causes acid rain and makes breathing difficult

super volcano a massive volcanic eruption which ejects at least 1,000 cubic kilometres of material

tectonic plates the parts into which the earth's crust and upper mantle are broken up and which move around independently creating volcanoes and earthquakes

tephra fragments of magma ejected from a volcano in an explosive eruption

tsunami a sea wave caused by earthquakes, volcanoes or landslides

FURTHER INFORMATION

Books

Claybourne, Anna, *Volcanoes: Discover the earth-shattering Power of the World's Volcanic Hotspots*, Kingfisher Books Ltd., 2007

Greenwood, Rosie, *I Wonder Why Volcanoes Blow Their Tops and Other Questions About Natural Disasters (I Wonder Why)*, Kingfisher Books Ltd., 2004

Kalman, Bobbie, *Volcanoes on earth (Looking at Earth)*, Crabtree Publishing Company, 2008

Levy, Matthys, *Earthquakes, Volcanoes, and Tsunamis: Projects for Beginning Geologists*, Chicago Review Press, 2009

Rubin, Ken, *Volcanoes & Earthquakes (Insiders)*, Simon & Schuster Children's Publishing, 2007

Spilsbury, Louise and Richard, *Violent Volcanoes (Awesome Forces of Nature)*, Heinemann Library, 2005

Stewart, Melissa, *Earthquakes and Volcanoes (FYI: For Your Information)*, Collins, 2008

Waldron, Melanie, and Lapthorn, Nicholas, *Volcanoes (Mapping Earthforms)*, Heinemann Library, 2007

Winchester, Simon, and Zimmermann, Dwight Jon, *The Day the World Exploded: The Earthshaking Catastrophe at Krakatoa*, Collins, 2008

DVD

Natural Disasters, DK Eyewitness Books, 2009

Websites

There are many websites that tell you about volcanoes. These are just some:

http://dsc.discovery.com/convergence/pompeii/pompeii.html
Find out about the Vesuvius eruption in 79 CE.

http://earthobservatory.nasa.gov/NaturalHazards/
NASA satellite images of volcanoes.

http://kids.discovery.com/games/pompeii/pompeii.html
Learn about tectonic plates and different types of volcanos. Look inside a volcano. Build a volcano.

http://science.howstuffworks.com/volcano.htm
Find out how volcanoes work and look at some exciting pictures in the image gallery.

http://volcano.oregonstate.edu/kids/index.html
This website includes games, virtual field trips and great photos.

http://www.fema.gov/kids/volcano.htm
This website contains volcano facts, information on mapping lava, Mount St Helens and measuring explosivity.

http://www.nationalgeographic.com/eye/volcanoes/volcanoes.html
This site includes information on volcanic effects and phenomena, interviews on Montserrat, videos of Mount St Helens and information on predicting volcanoes.

http://www.pbs.org/wnet/savageearth/volcanoes/index.html
Find out about volcanoes of North America, on Montserrat and on other planets. The site also shows a fun animation of an eruption.

http://www.weatherwizkids.com/volcano1.htm
Discover facts about volcanoes and plate tectonics.

INDEX